SWEAR WORD COLORING BOOK FOR ADULTS

THIS BOOK BELONGS TO

____

First Printing, 2019

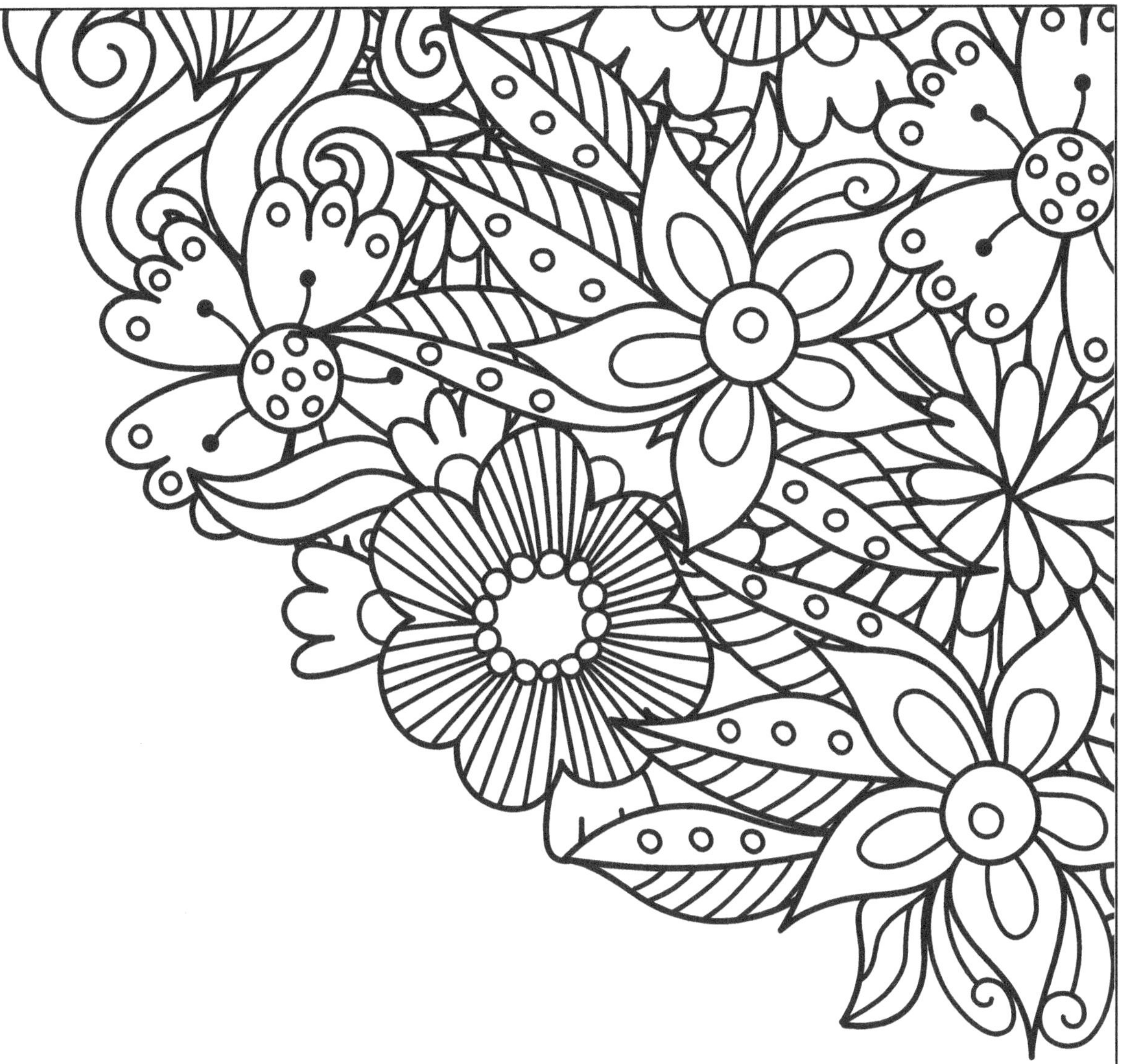

fuck you!

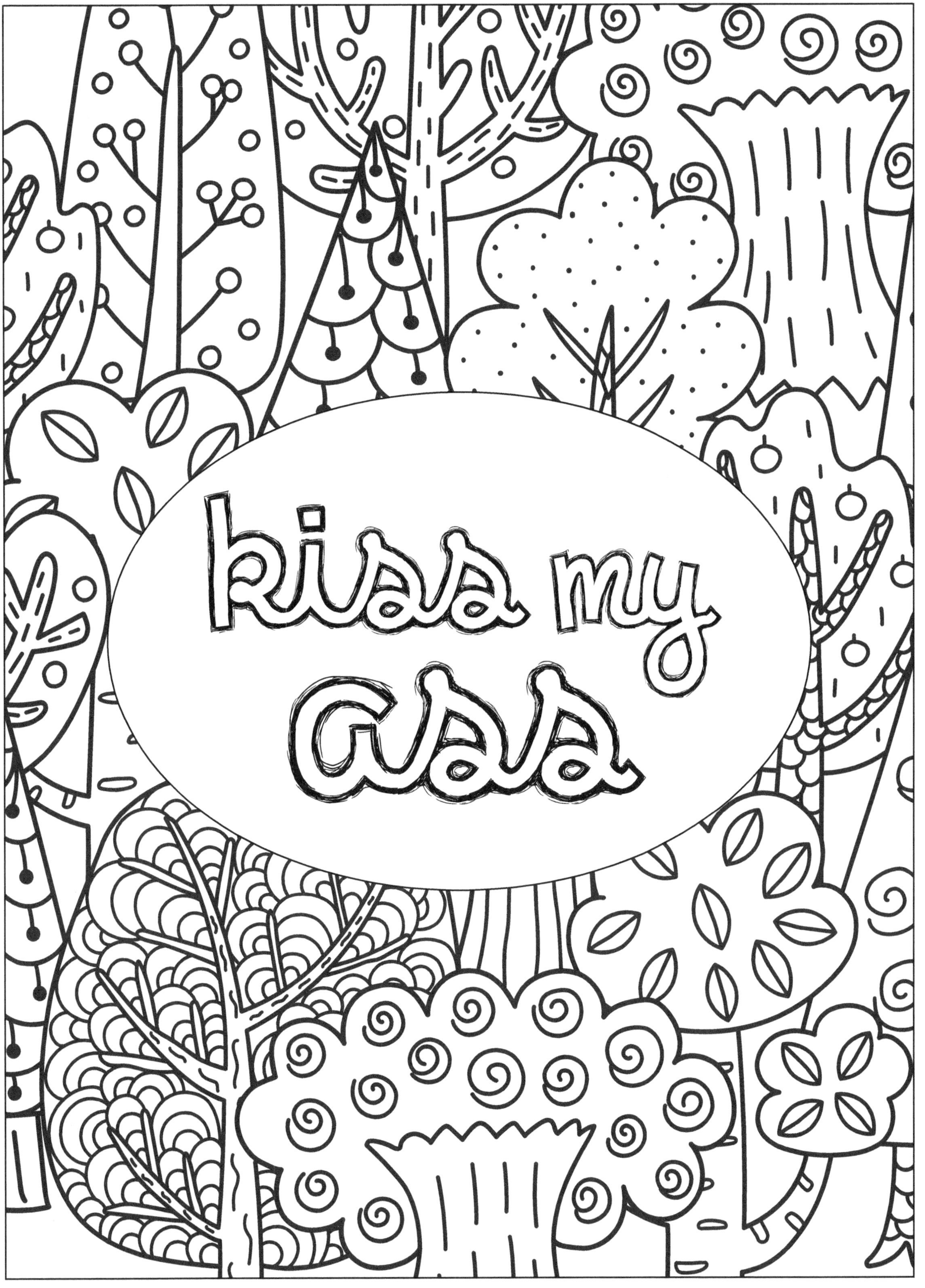
kiss my
ass

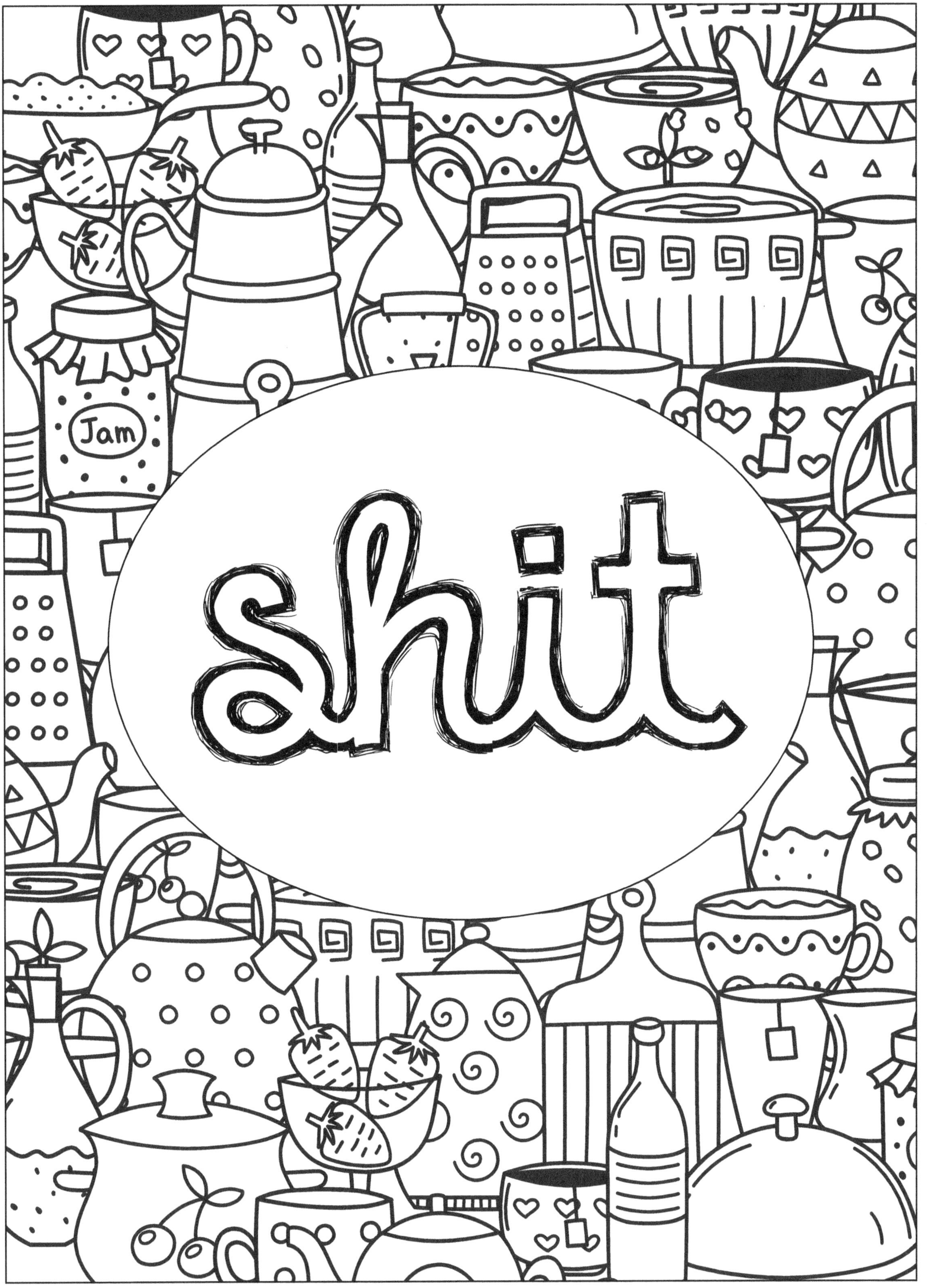
Jam
shit

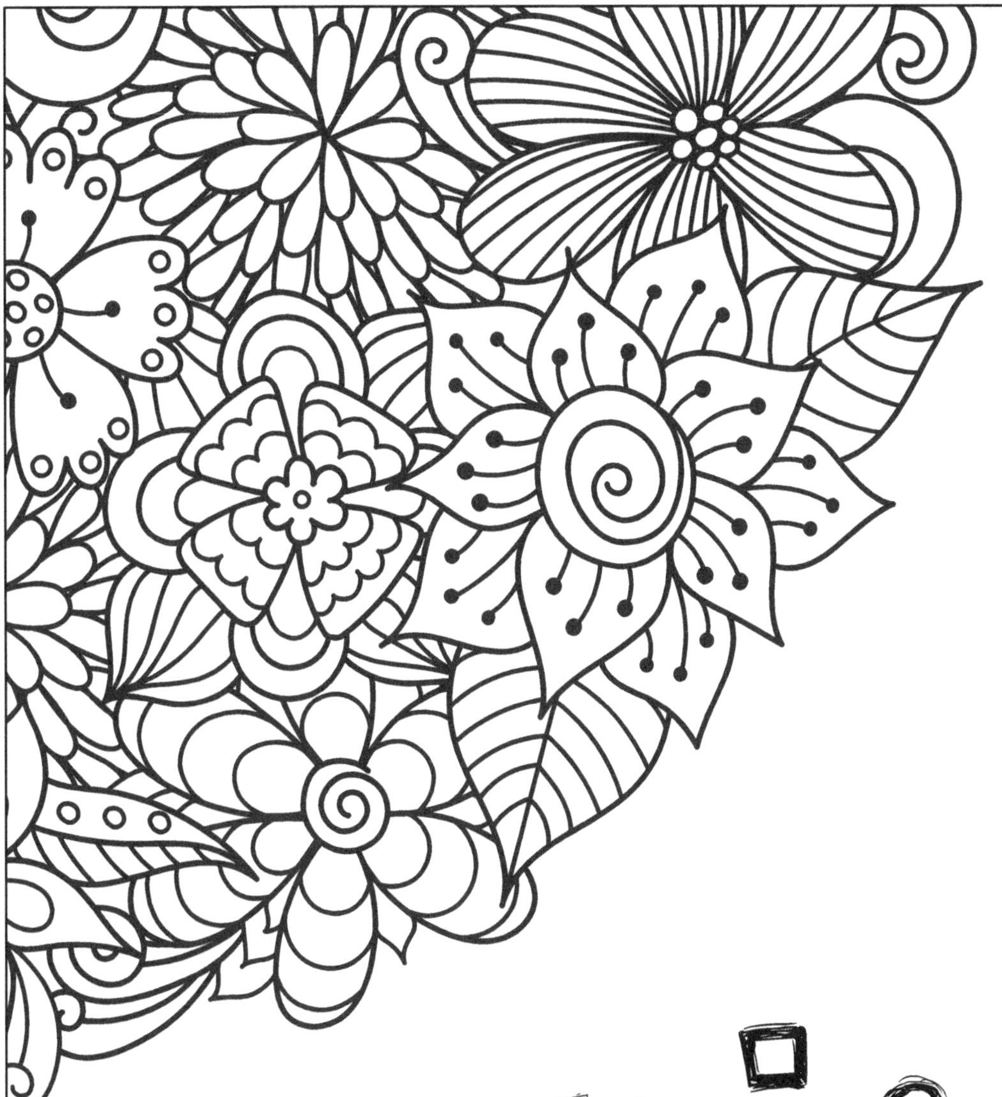

piss
off

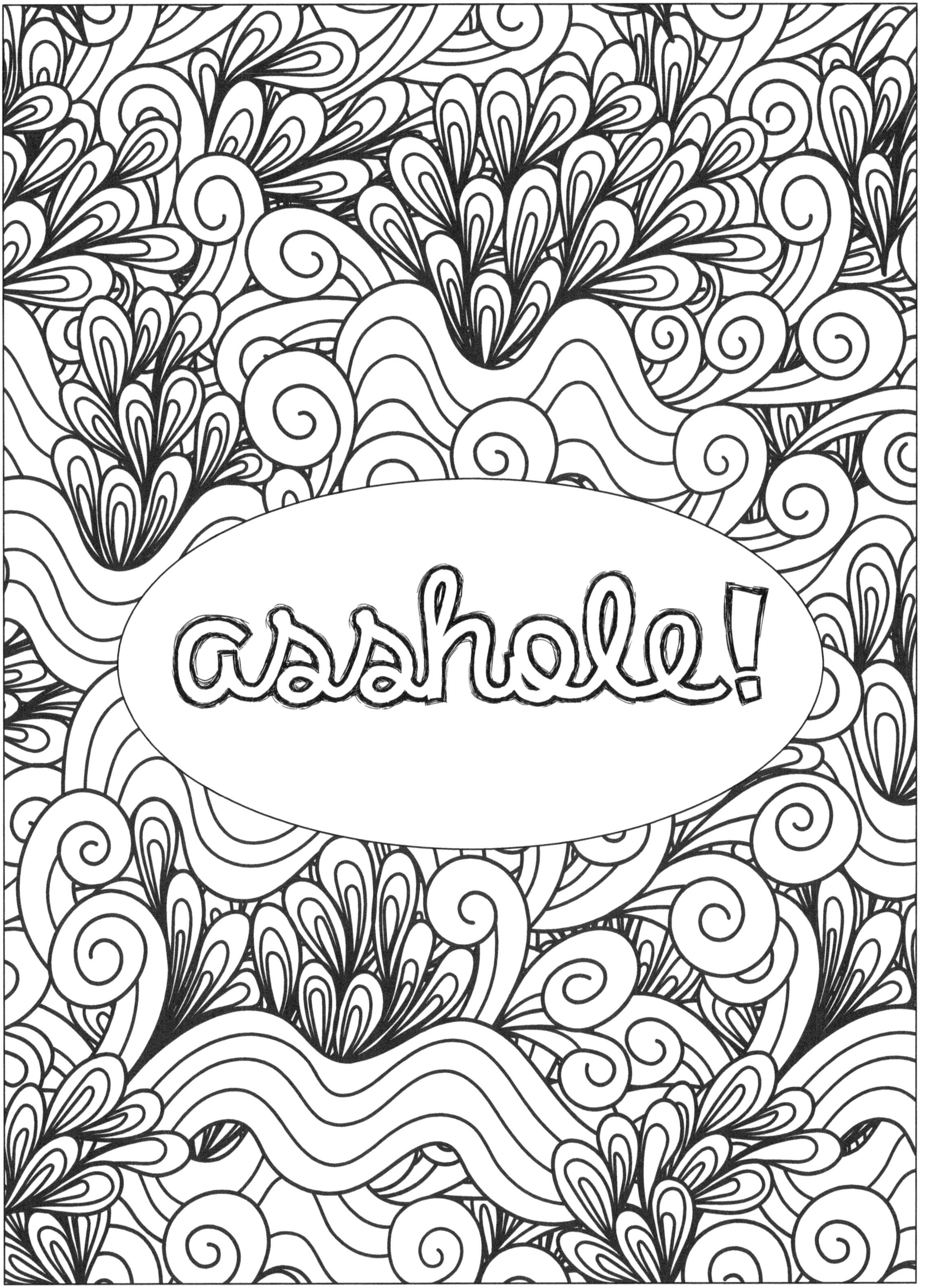
asshole!

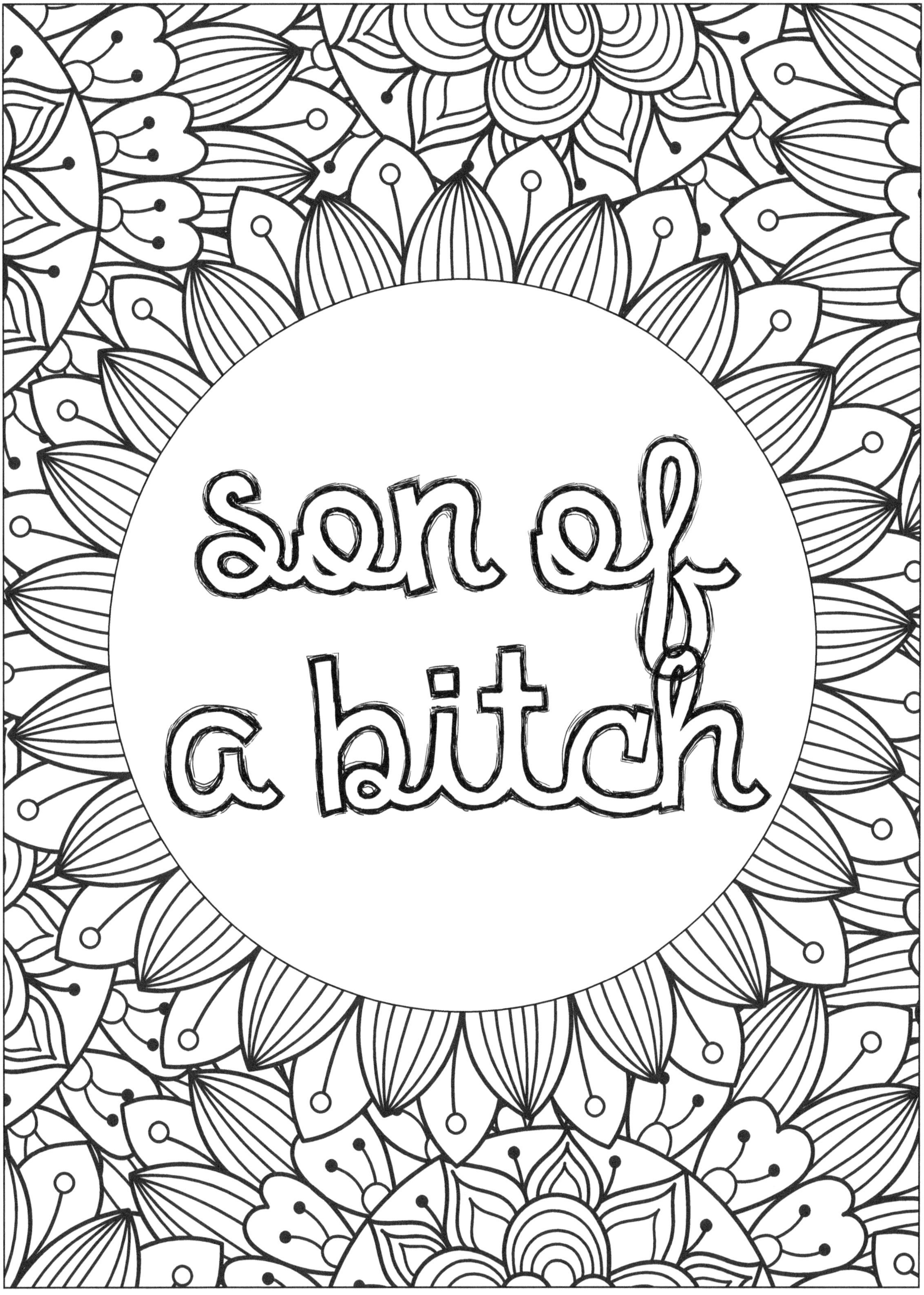
son of
a bitch

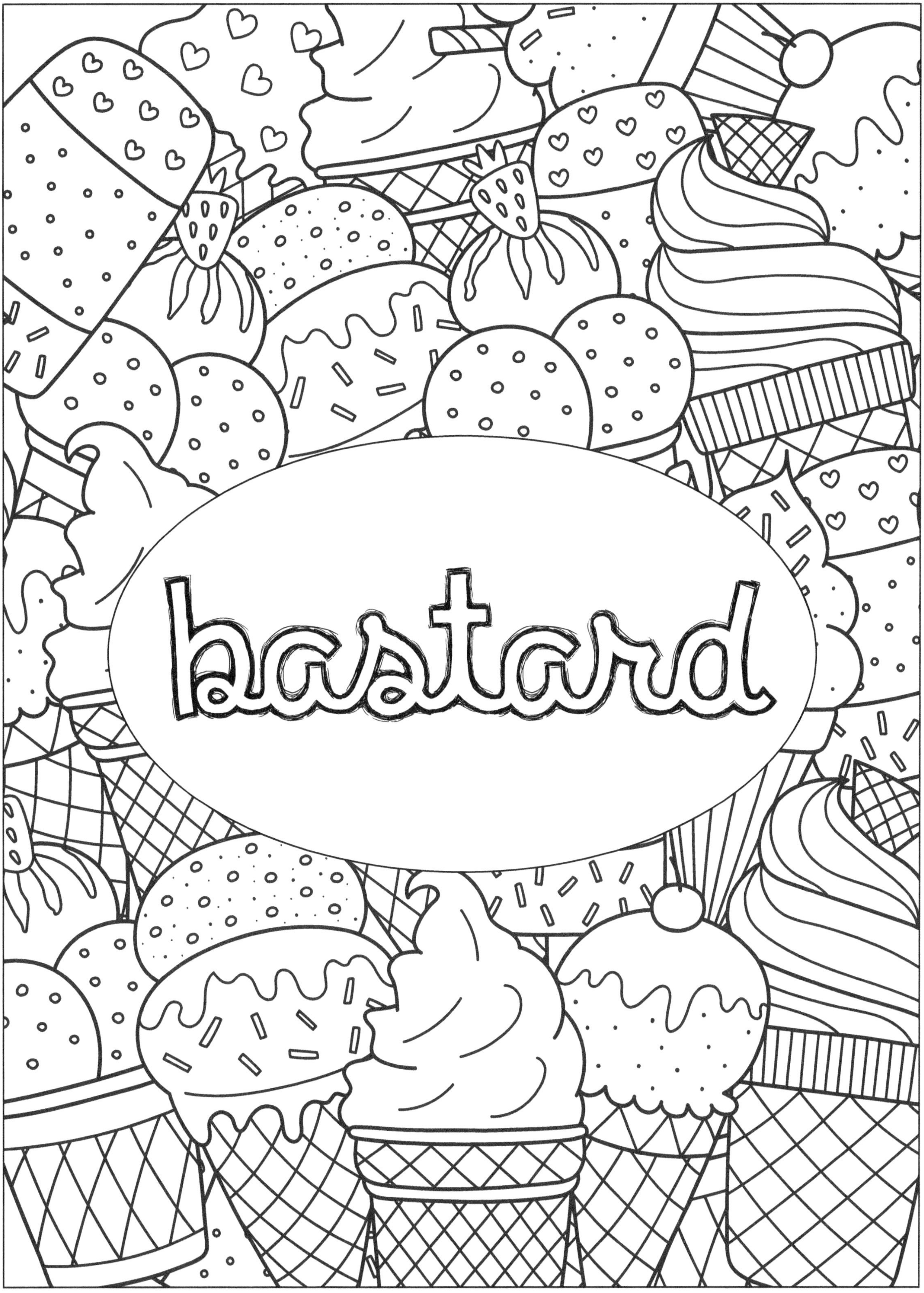
bastard

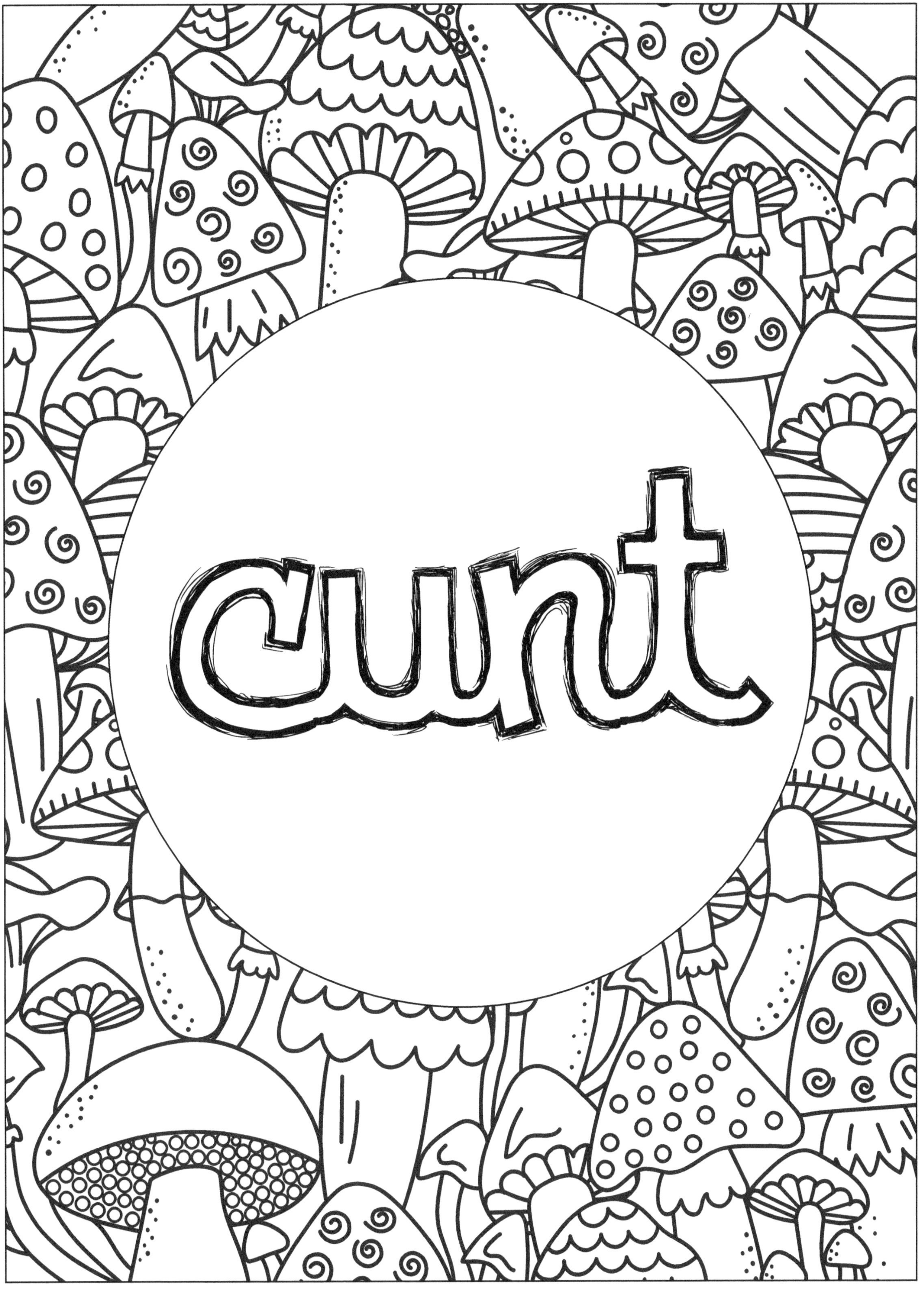
cunt

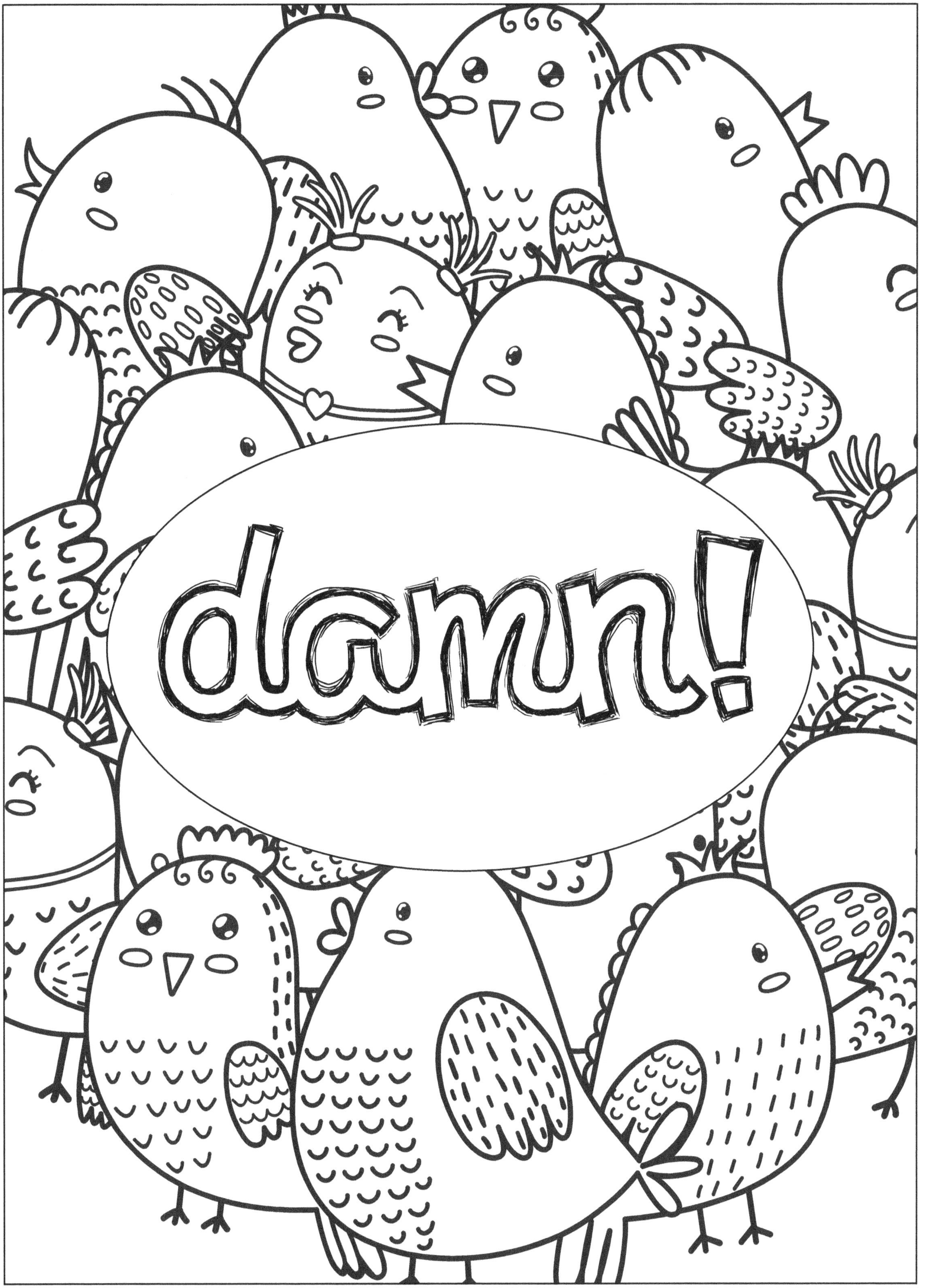
damn!

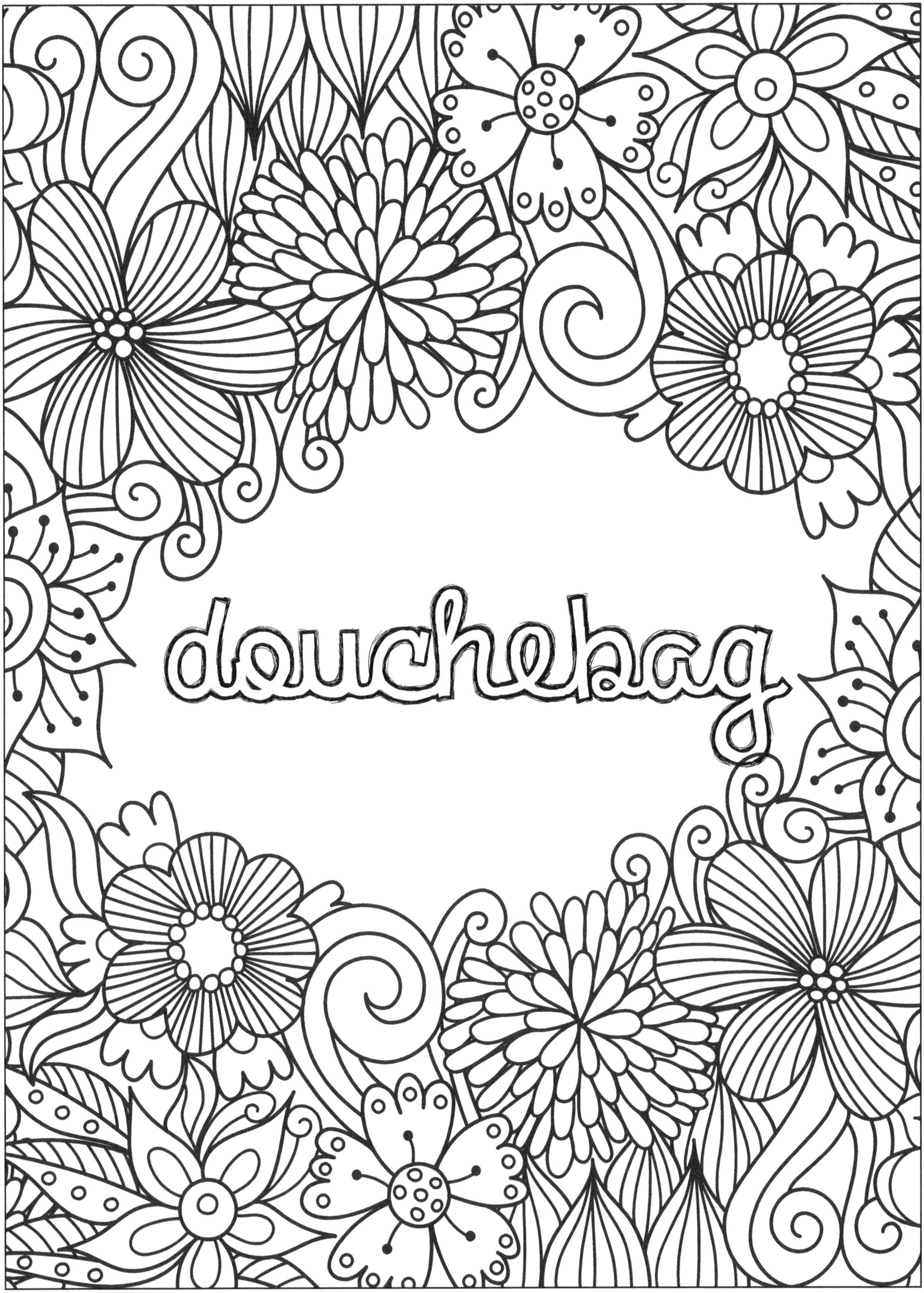
douchebag

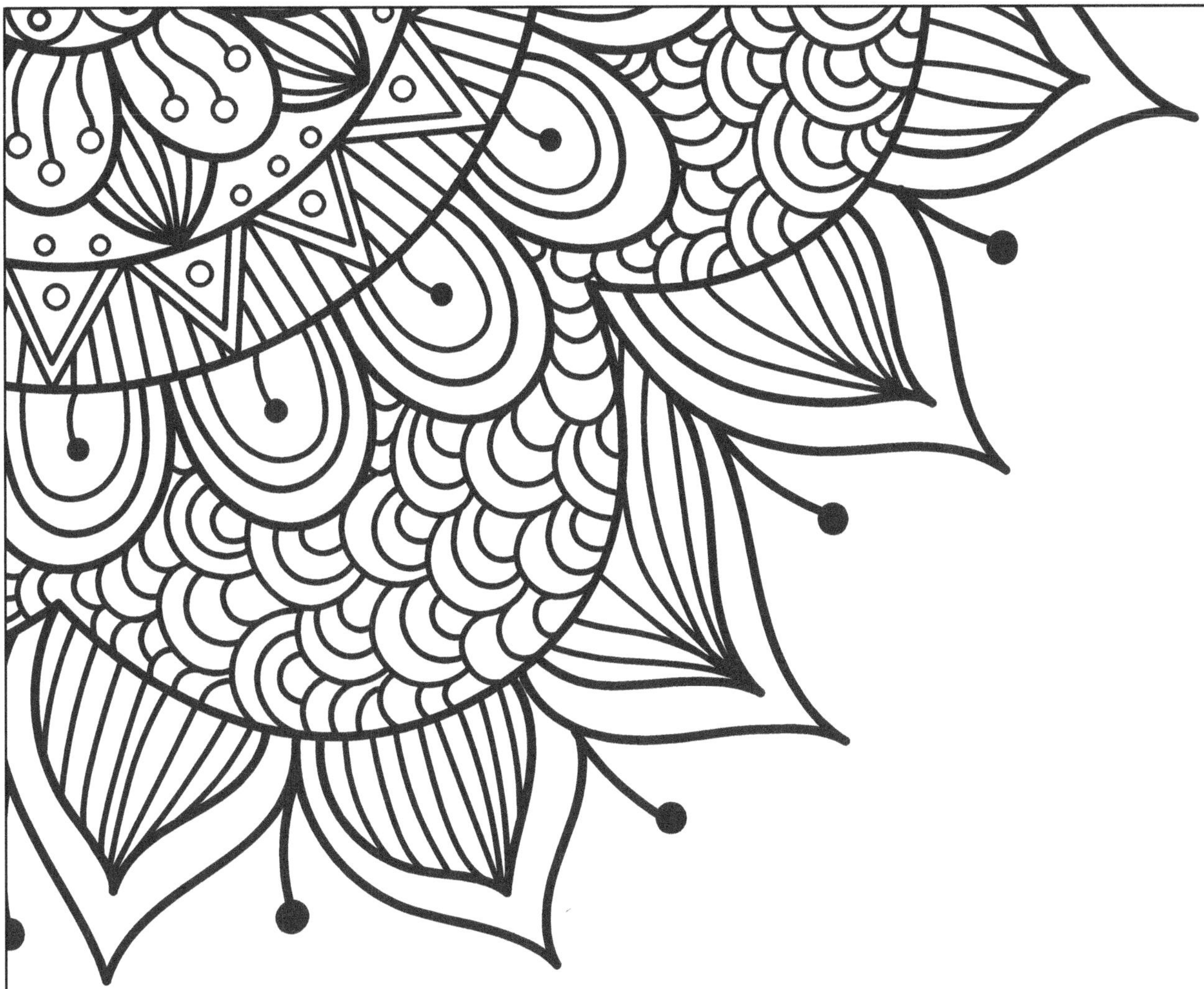

bitch

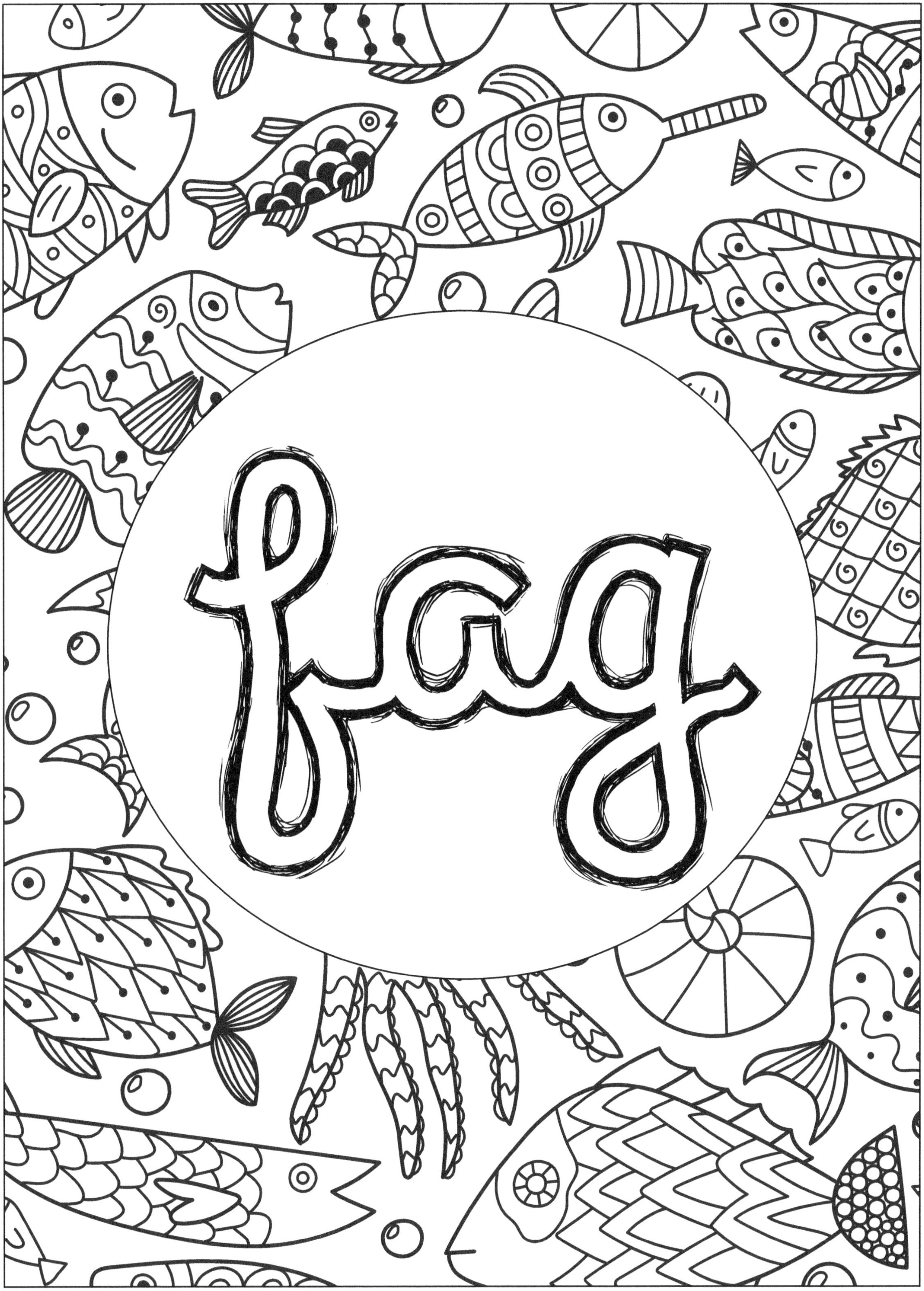
fag

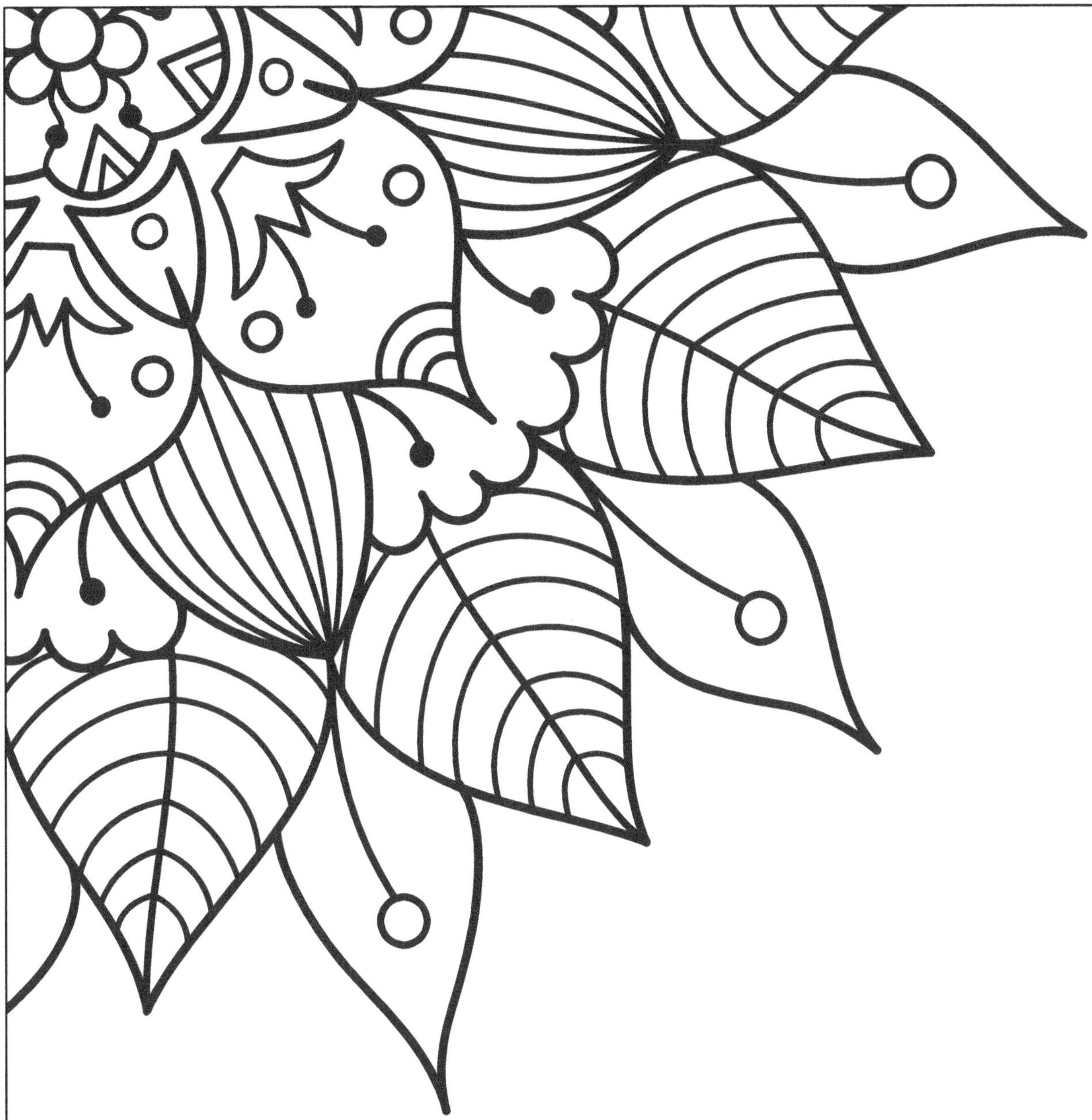

whore!

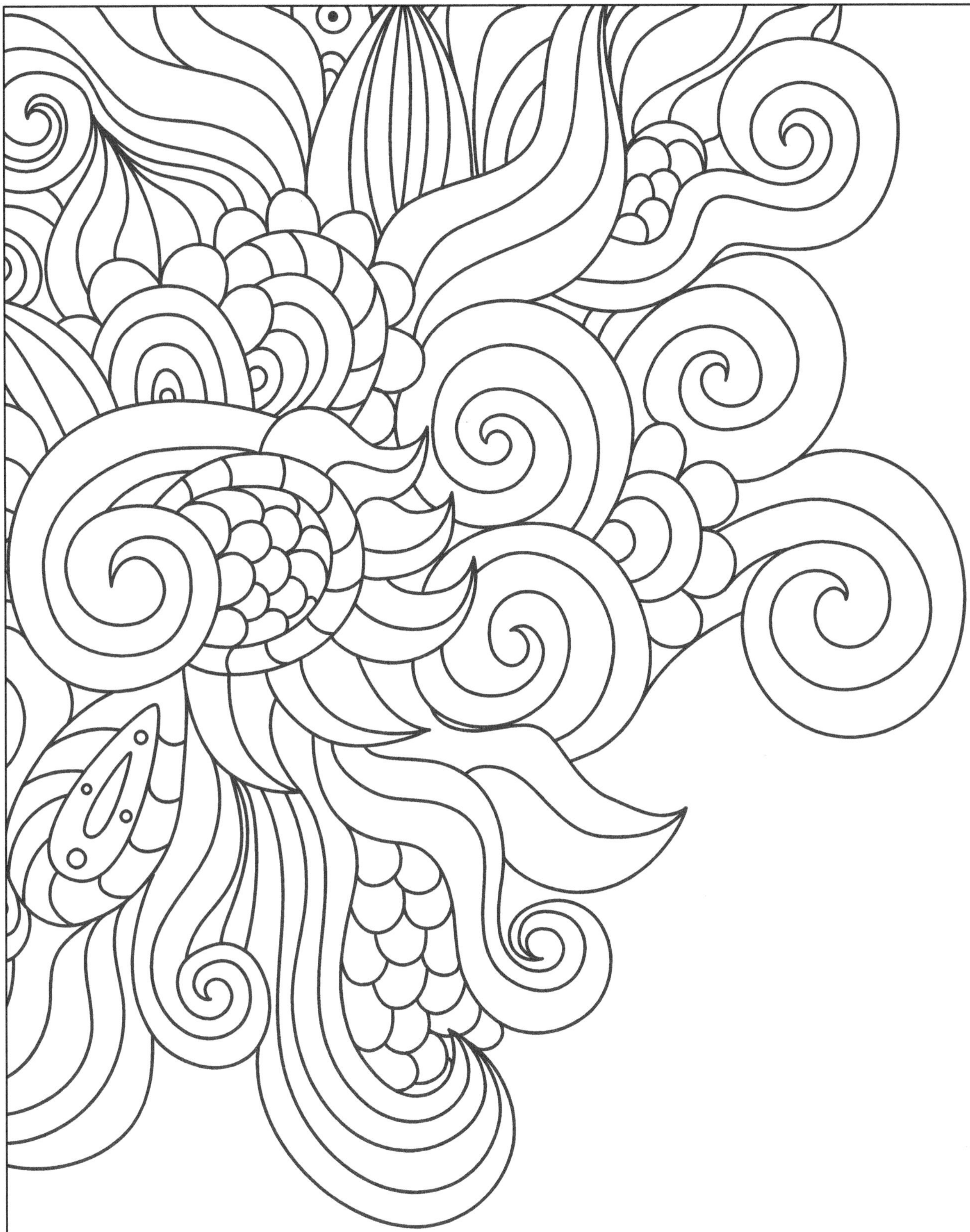

jerkoff!

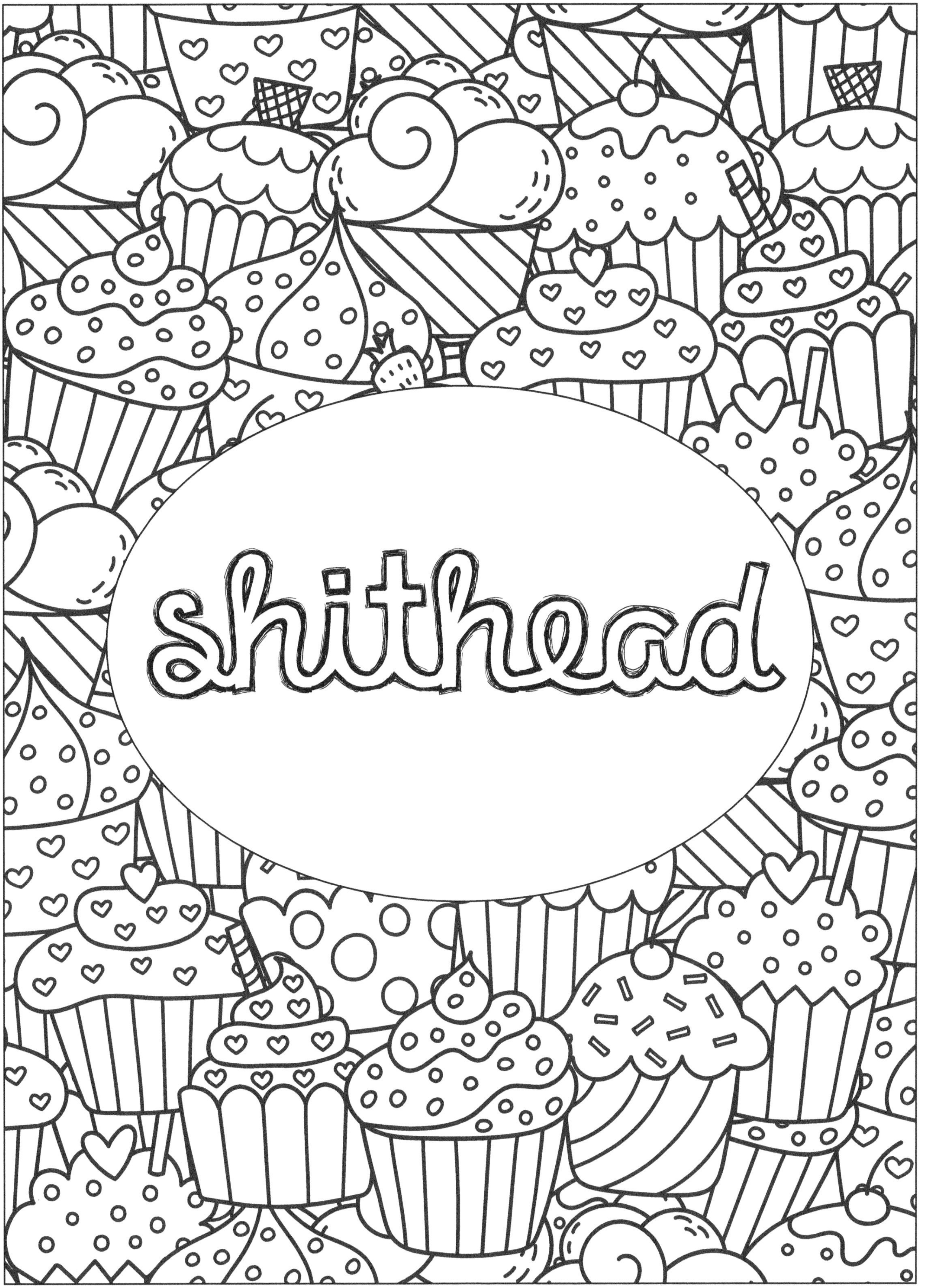
shithead

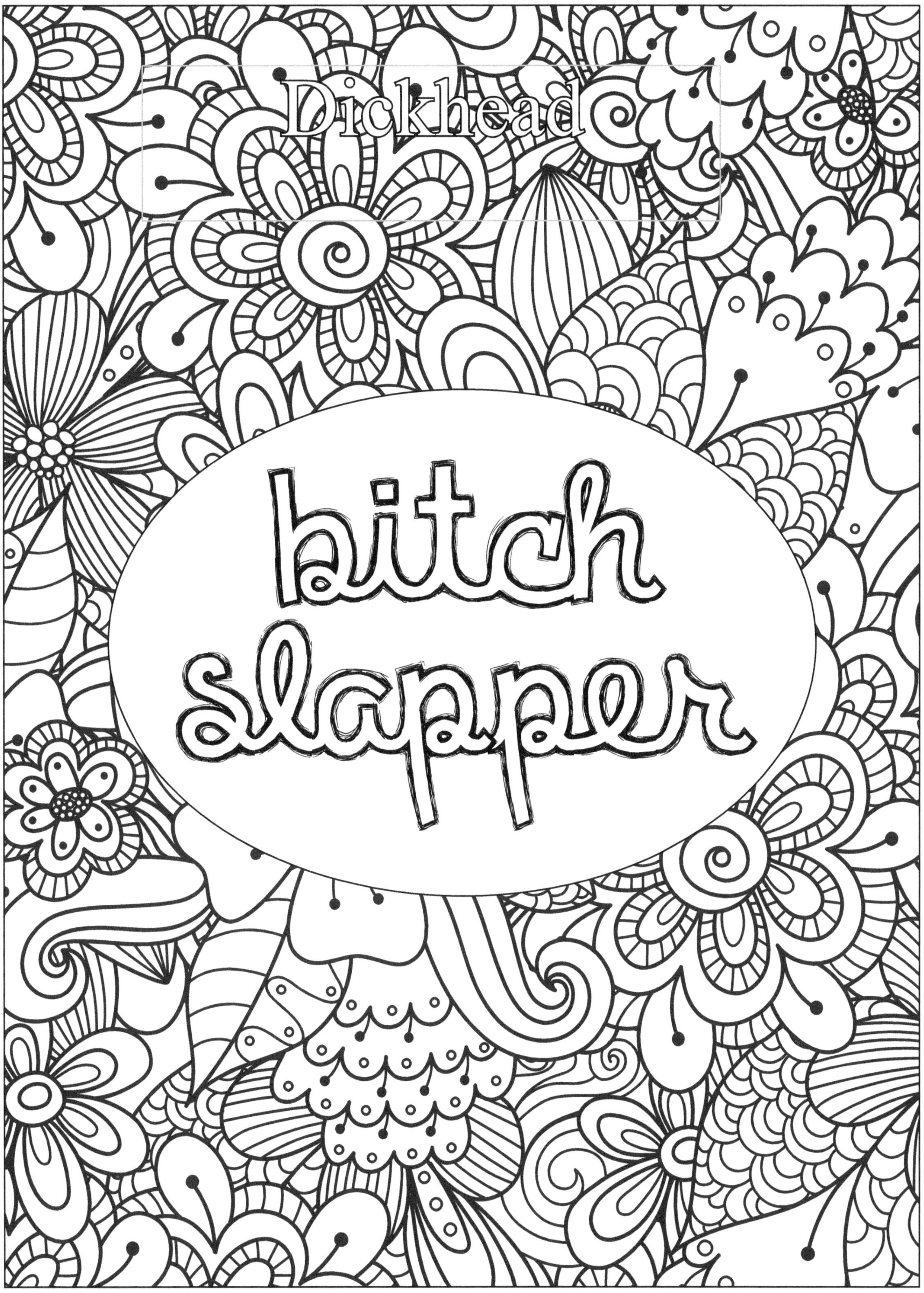
Dickhead
bitch slapper

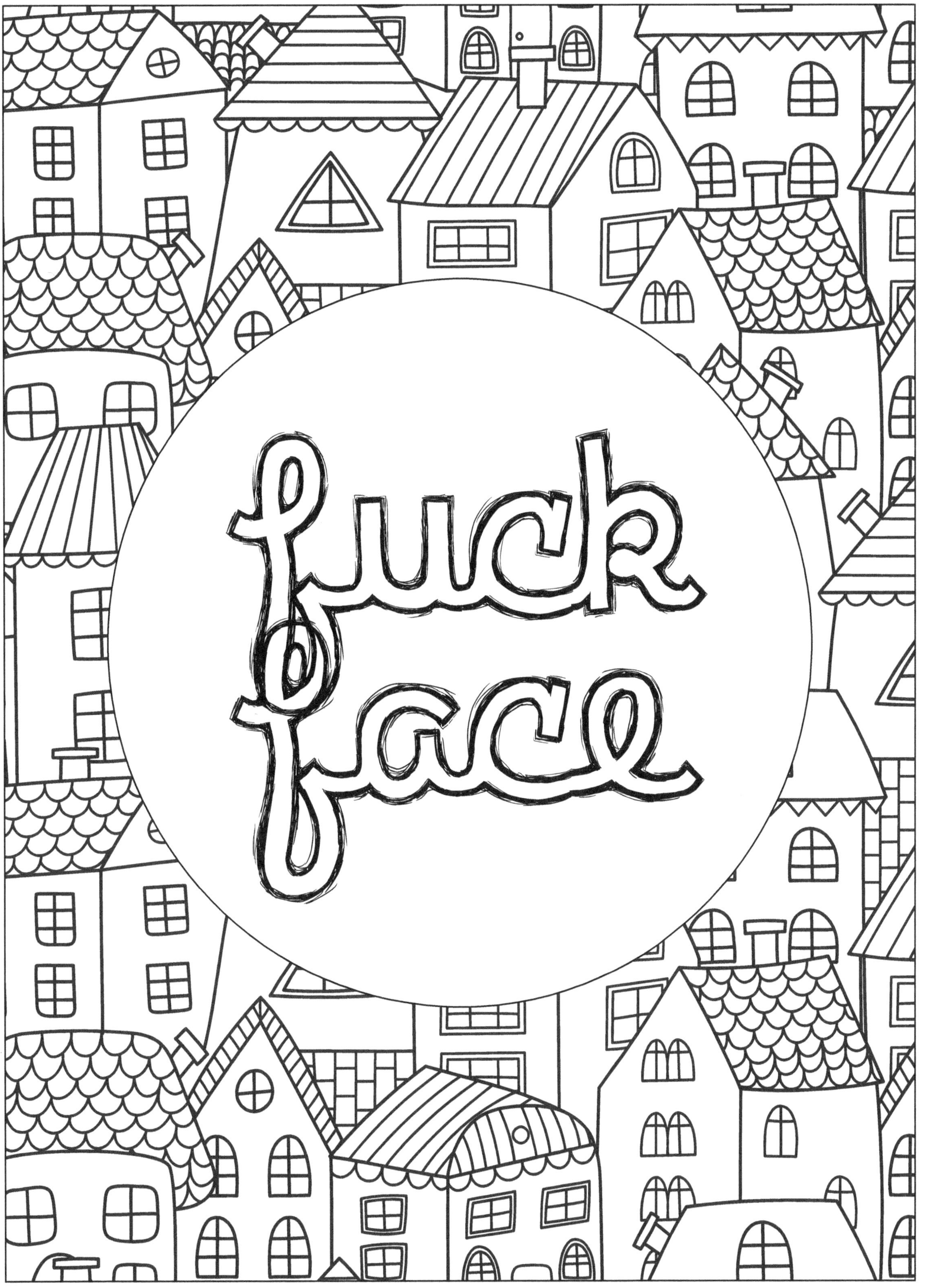
fuck face

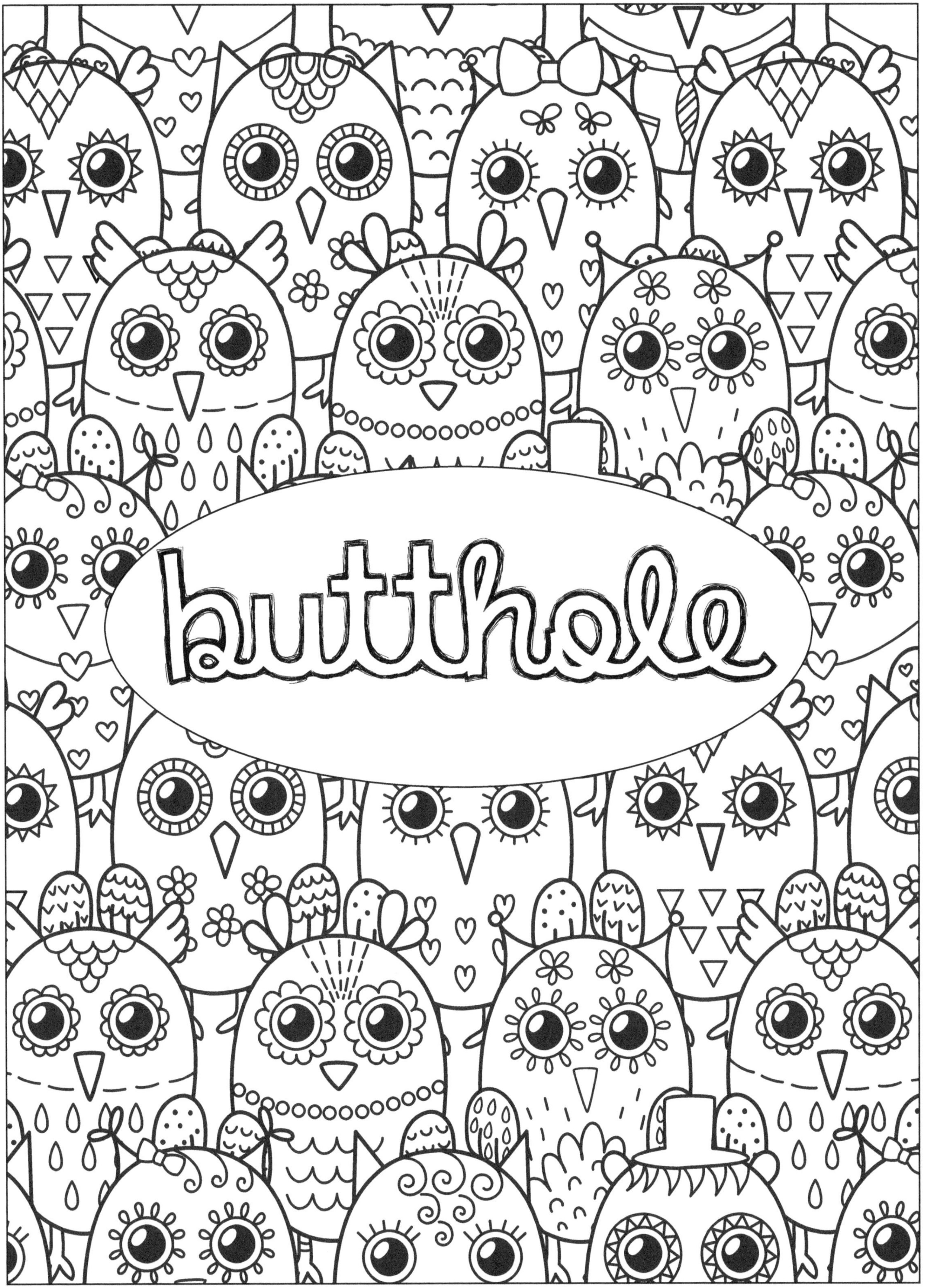
butthole

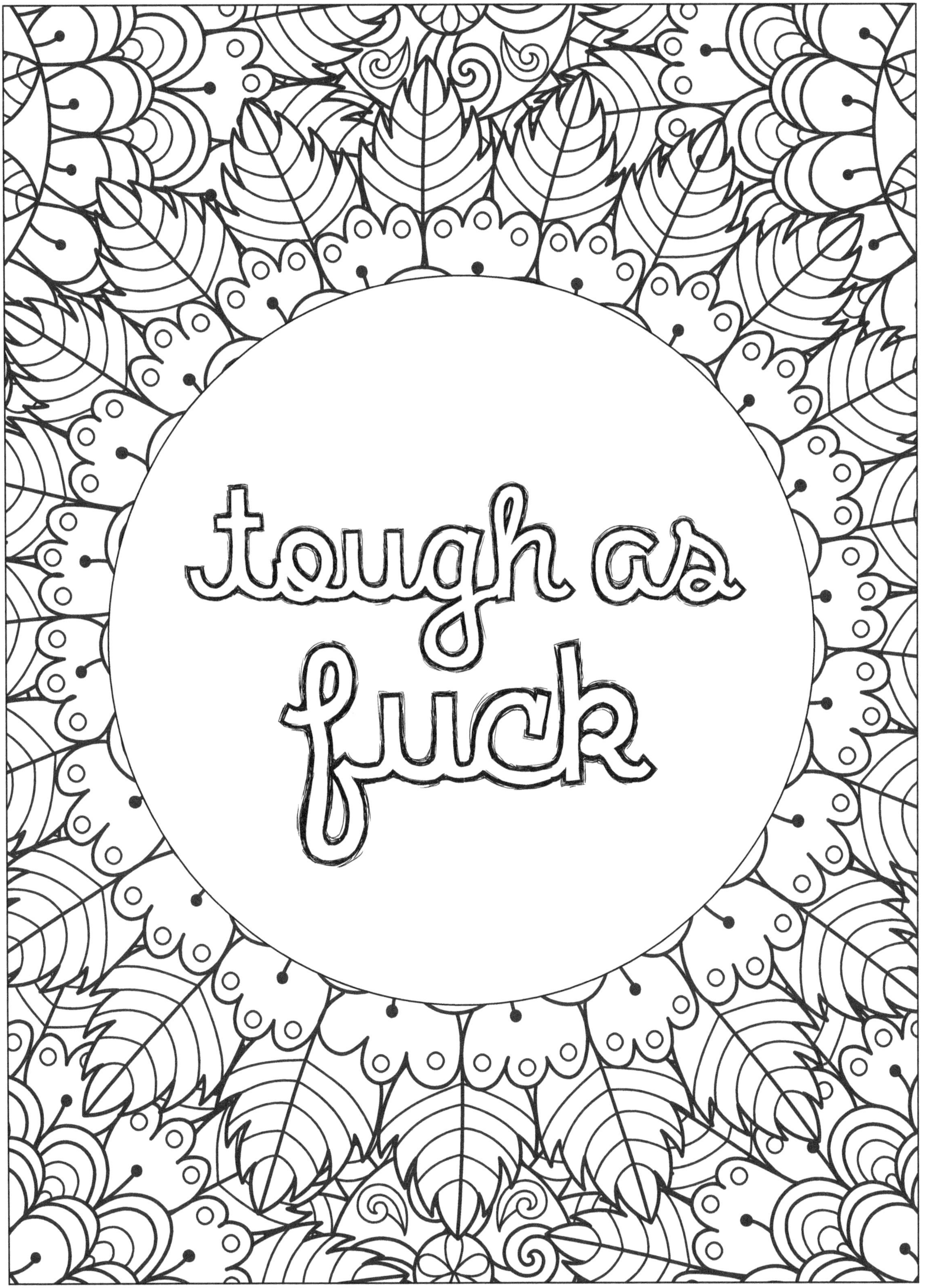
tough as
fuck

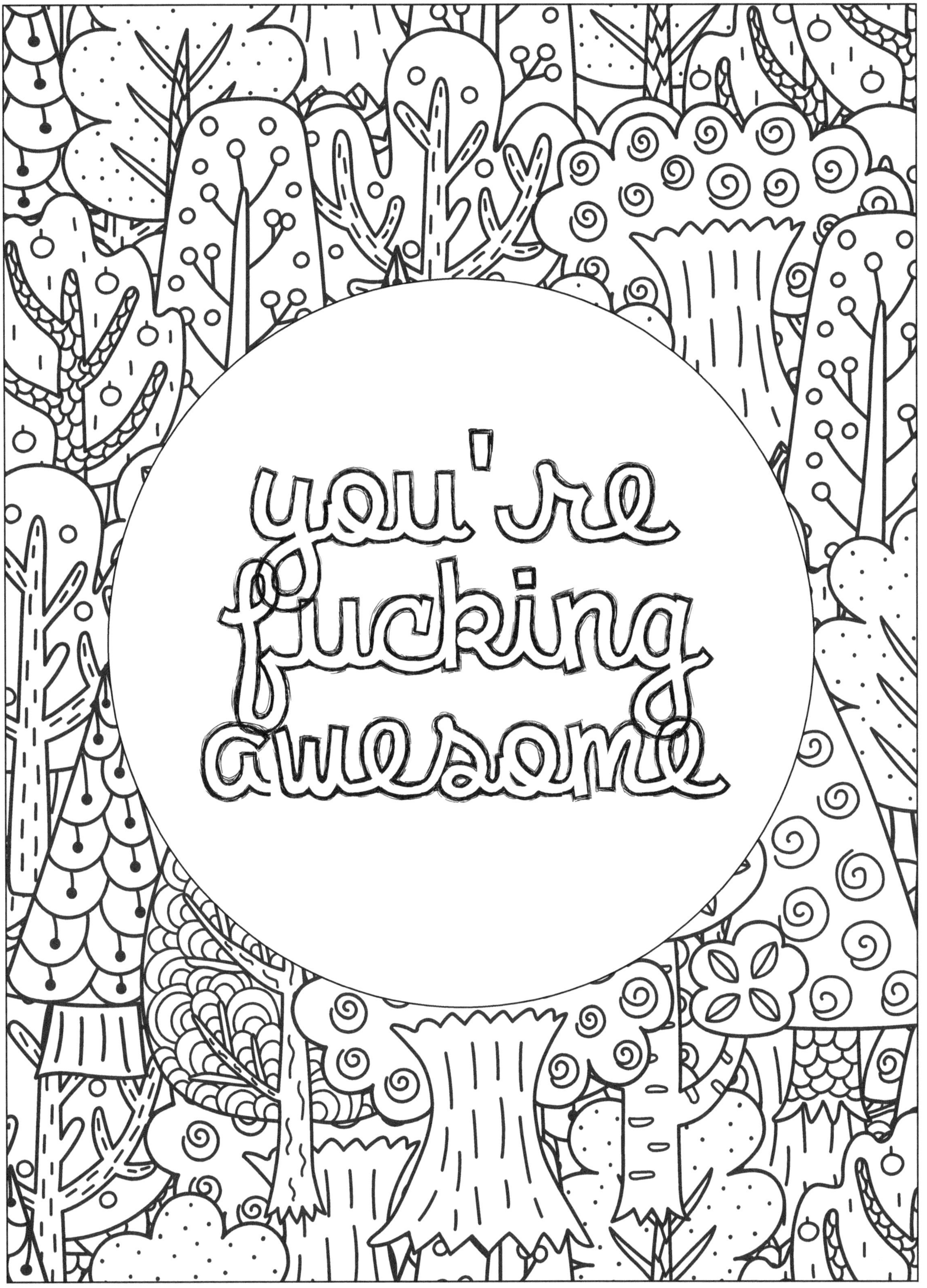
you're
fucking
awesome

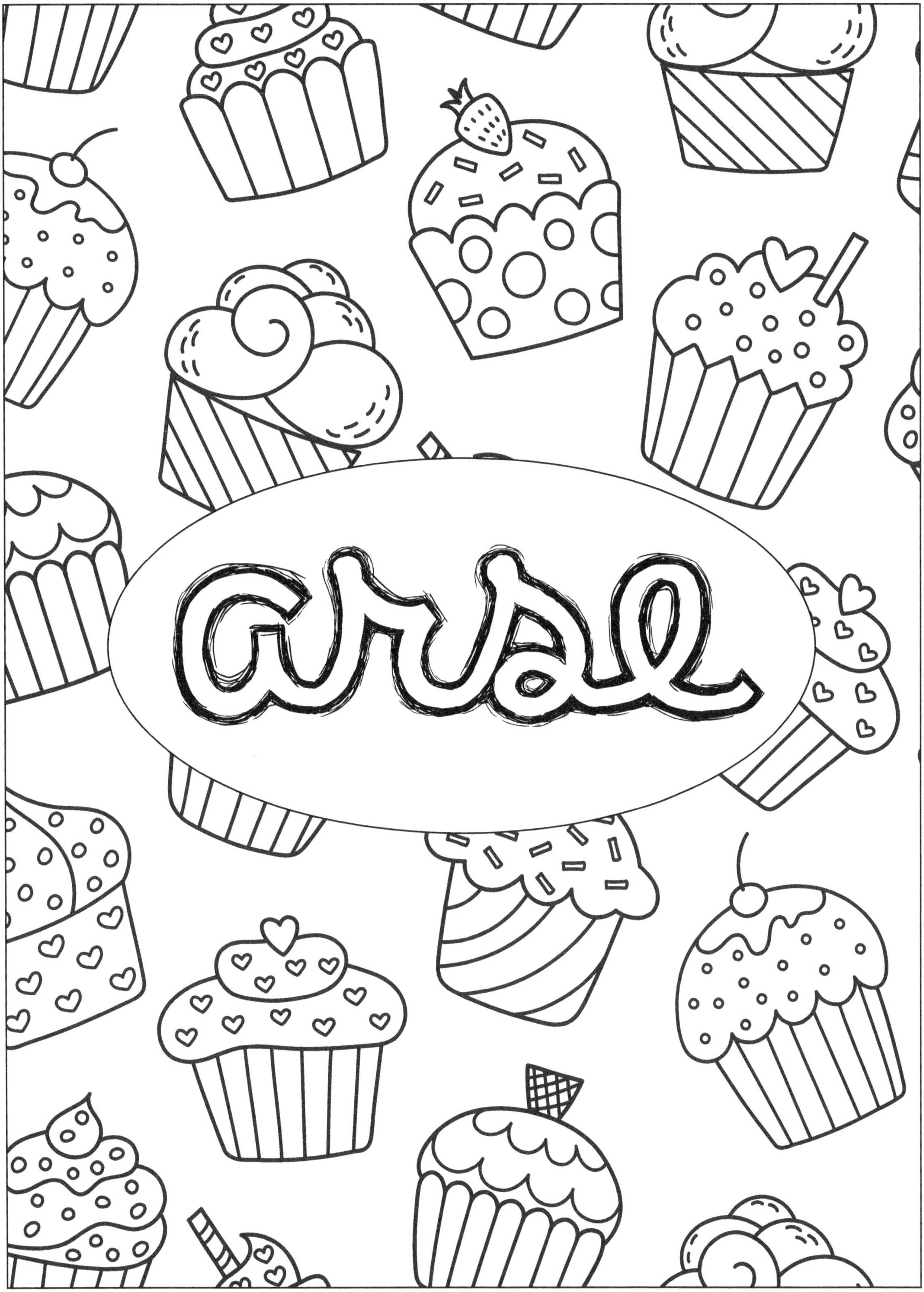
arse

ballsucker

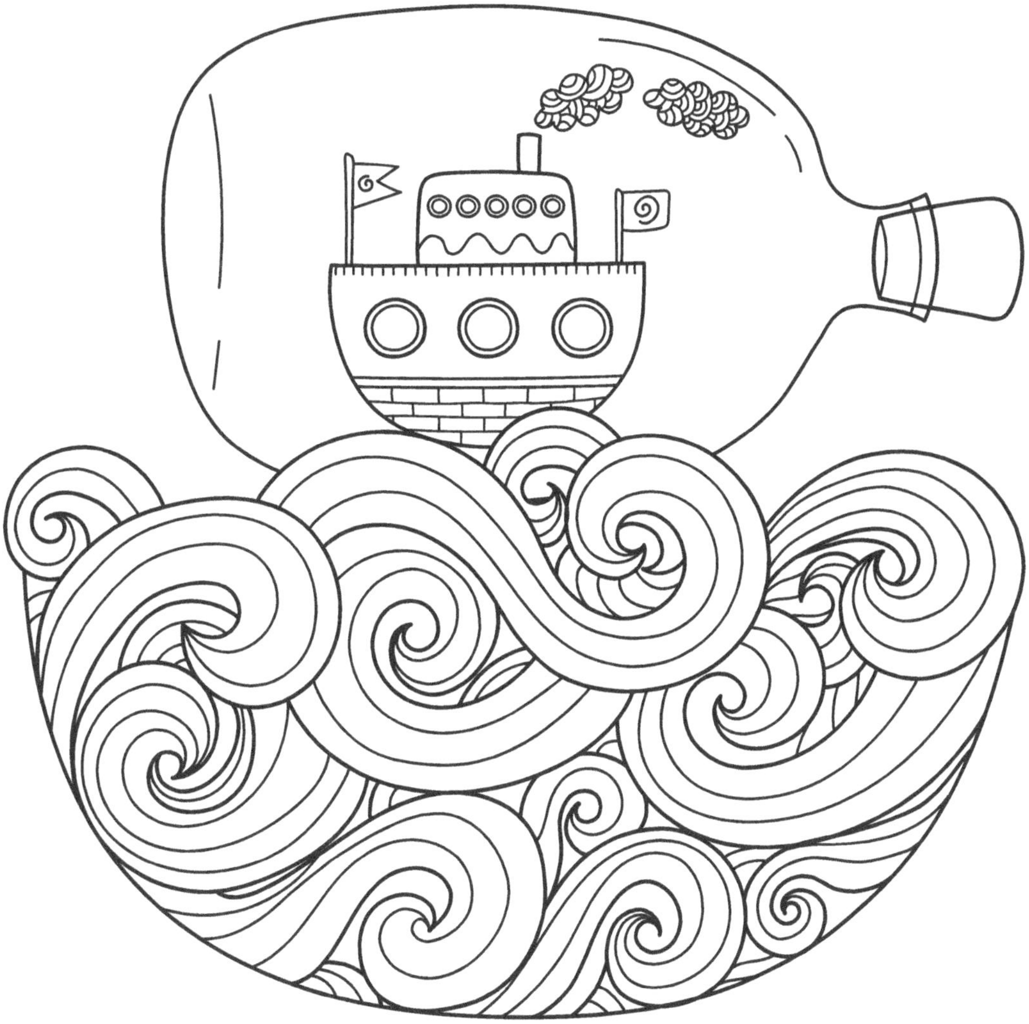

faceass

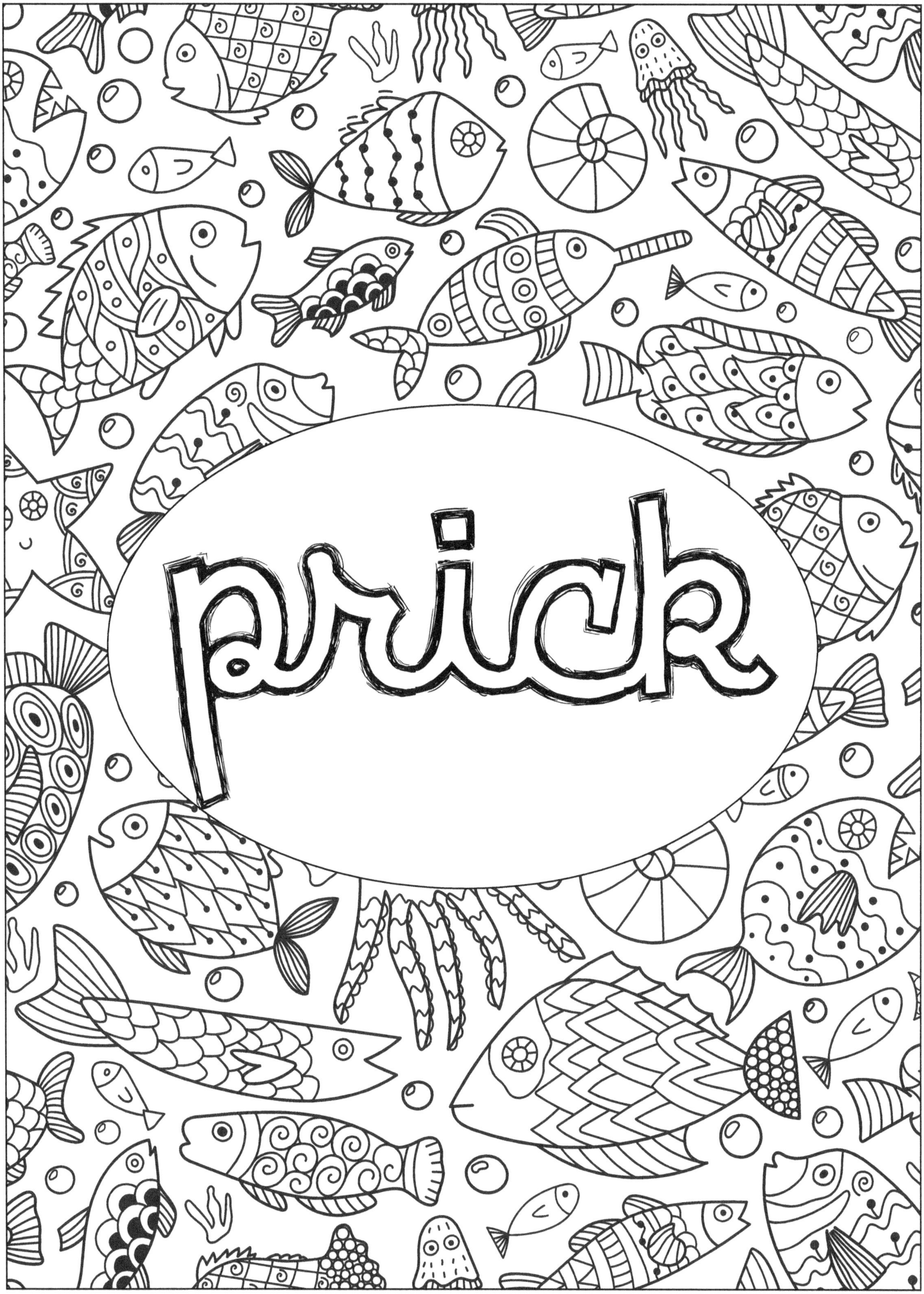
prick

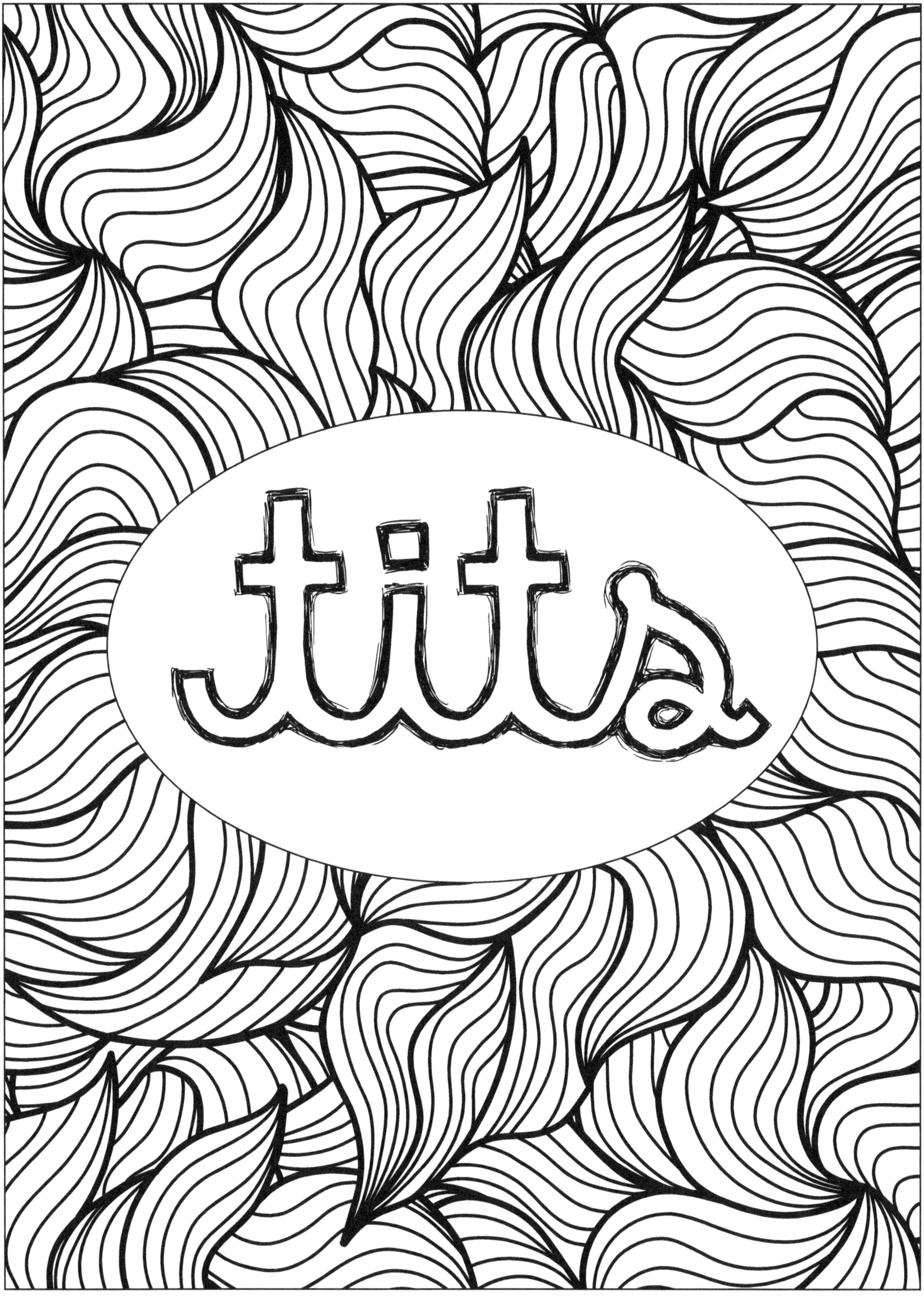
tits

www.ingramcontent.com/pod-product-compliance
Lightning Source LLC
Chambersburg PA
CBHW080849170526
45158CB00009B/2679
* 9 7 8 1 0 8 1 2 8 0 8 1 9 *